BEHAVE LIKE A RICH MAN

AHMED EL KASHEF

Table of Contents

Introduction: The Rich Man's Mindset
- Understanding Wealth Beyond Money
- The Power of Thinking Big
- Why Behavior Defines Success

Chapter 1: Think Abundantly
- Shifting from Scarcity to Abundance
- The Importance of Optimism in Building Wealth
- How to Train Your Brain to See Opportunities
- Action Step: Begin Shifting Your Mindset

Chapter 2: Embrace Long-Term Thinking
- Delayed Gratification: A Wealthy Man's Skill
- Thinking in Decades, Not Days
- Building Patience and Persistence for Lasting Success
- Why Short-Term Thinking Holds People Back
- How to Develop a Long-Term Perspective
- Action Step: Start Thinking Long-Term

Chapter 3: Confidence and Self-Worth

- Believing in Yourself as an Investment
- How to Build Unshakeable Confidence
- The Role of Self-Worth in Financial Success
- How to Increase Your Self-Worth
- The Wealthy Approach to Negotiation
- Action Step: Build Your Confidence and Self-Worth

Chapter 4: Daily Habits of the Wealthy

- The Power of Routine
- Key Habits of the Wealthy
- Developing Discipline Through Consistency
- Building Wealth through Small Daily Actions
- The Wealthy Mindset: Abundance vs. Scarcity
- Action Step: Evaluate Your Daily Habits

Chapter 5: Financial Literacy and Money Management

- Understanding Financial Literacy
- Key Components of Financial Literacy
- Building a Strong Money Management Strategy
- The Role of Advisors and Mentors
- Action Step: Assess Your Financial Literacy

Chapter 6: The Mindset of Wealth and Abundance

- The Power of Mindset
- Cultivating an Abundance Mindset
- Embracing Risk and Failure
- Visualization and Goal Setting
- Action Step: Assess Your Mindset

Chapter 7: Networking and Building Wealthy Relationships

- The Power of Networking
- Strategies for Effective Networking
- Building Wealthy Relationships
- Networking Mindset: Be Open to Opportunities
- Action Step: Evaluate Your Network

Chapter 8: Investment Strategies for Wealth Building

- Understanding Investment Basics
- Types of Investments
- Building an Investment Strategy
- Investing for the Long Term
- Action Step: Develop Your Investment Plan

Chapter 9: Personal Branding and Marketing Yourself for Success

- The Importance of Personal Branding
- Building Your Personal Brand
- Marketing Yourself Effectively

- Maintaining Your Personal Brand
- Action Step: Craft Your Personal Brand Statement

Chapter 10: Financial Literacy and Education for Wealth Creation

- The Importance of Financial Literacy
- Key Components of Financial Literacy
- Continuous Education and Self-Improvement
- Action Step: Create a Financial Literacy Plan

Chapter 11: Setting Financial Goals and Creating Action Plans

- The Importance of Financial Goal Setting
- Types of Financial Goals
- Creating SMART Goals
- Developing an Action Plan
- Action Step: Define Your Financial Goals

Chapter 12: Resilience and Adaptability in Financial Success

- The Role of Resilience in Wealth Building
- The Importance of Adaptability
- Building Resilience and Adaptability
- Learning from Setbacks
- Action Step: Cultivate Your Resilience and Adaptability

Chapter 13: Personal Development and Lifelong Learning for Wealth Sustainability

- The Link Between Personal Development and Financial Success
- The Importance of Lifelong Learning
- Strategies for Personal Development and Lifelong Learning
- Cultivating a Growth Mindset
- Action Step: Commit to Personal Development

Chapter 14: The Significance of Giving Back and Community Contribution

- The Impact of Philanthropy on Wealth
- The Benefits of Community Involvement
- Ways to Give Back and Get Involved
- Integrating Philanthropy into Your Financial Planning
- Action Step: Commit to Giving Back

Chapter 15: The Significance of Maintaining a Balanced Life and Well-Being

- The Connection Between Well-Being and Financial Success
- The Importance of Life Balance

- Strategies for Maintaining Balance and Well-Being
- Maintaining Financial Well-Being
- Action Step: Commit to a Balanced Life

Introduction: The Rich Man's Mindset

Wealth is more than just a number in a bank account; it is a way of thinking, behaving, and living. True wealth begins in the mind long before it is reflected in material possessions or financial statements. Those who accumulate and sustain wealth approach life differently—they see opportunities where others see obstacles, invest in personal growth when others remain stagnant, and think in terms of long-term gain rather than immediate reward. In this book, we explore what it truly means to behave like a rich man, not just by adopting the outward trappings of wealth, but by embodying the mindset that creates it.

Understanding Wealth Beyond Money

Too often, we limit our definition of wealth to financial resources, but true wealth encompasses much more. It includes not only money but also freedom, health, relationships, knowledge, and peace of mind. A rich man understands that the most valuable resources are intangible—time, energy, and focus. These are things that money cannot buy, and yet they are critical in building and sustaining financial success.

Wealth, at its core, is about options. The wealthiest people on the planet can choose where they live, how they spend their time, and what they focus on. They are not restricted by the same limitations as those living in scarcity. But this freedom is the result of a mindset that prioritizes long-term value over short-term indulgence, continuous learning over complacency, and strategic action over mere reaction.

By understanding wealth as a holistic concept, you begin to realize that financial success is just one piece of a larger puzzle. The goal is to live richly in all areas of life—not just to accumulate money, but to use it as a tool to build a life that is meaningful, fulfilling, and free.

The Power of Thinking Big

The ability to think big is a hallmark of the wealthy mindset. Many people limit their ambitions based on their current circumstances, but the rich do the opposite: they envision what seems impossible and work backward to make it happen. They understand that big dreams require big plans, and big plans require bold actions. Thinking big isn't just about setting lofty goals—it's about breaking free from the mental limitations that hold most people back.

When you think small, you play small. Your actions are confined to what feels safe, familiar, and achievable within the boundaries of your present reality. But when you think big, you expand your possibilities. You begin to see the world as full of potential, where barriers become steppingstones, and the impossible becomes achievable.

The rich don't fear failure because they see it as part of the process of achieving greatness. They aren't afraid to take risks because they know that the greatest rewards often lie just beyond their comfort zones. By embracing the power of thinking big, they open themselves up to opportunities that most people never even imagine.

Why Behavior Defines Success

At the end of the day, it's not just about what you think or believe—it's about what you do. Behavior is what sets the rich apart from everyone else. It's easy to wish for wealth or dream of success, but without the discipline and habits to back it up, those dreams remain fantasies. The wealthy are characterized by their ability to turn their ambitions into actions, consistently and persistently over time.

Successful people behave in ways that align with their goals. They are disciplined in how they manage their time, energy, and resources. They develop habits that lead to long-term success, such as saving, investing, and learning. They understand the importance of relationships and the power of surrounding themselves with people who challenge and inspire them. Most importantly, they are committed to personal growth—they invest in themselves just as they would in a business or financial portfolio.

In this book, you will learn how to cultivate the mindset, habits, and behaviors of the rich. Each chapter will provide insights and strategies that, when applied consistently, will move you closer to the life of freedom, abundance, and wealth you desire. Remember, wealth is not just about money—it's about living a life that is rich in every sense. And it all starts with the right mindset.

Chapter 1: Think Abundantly

Shifting from Scarcity to Abundance

What separates the truly wealthy from others is not just the amount of money in their bank accounts, but their perspective on life, opportunity, and success. A rich man's journey to financial independence often begins with the same resources as anyone else, but their success lies in how they think.

The Scarcity Mindset

Many people are trapped in what is called the "scarcity mindset." This type of thinking focuses on limitations—there's never enough money, time, or resources to go around. Those with a scarcity mindset believe that opportunities are rare, and when they appear, they must be taken quickly, or they will be lost forever. This leads to a life of constant worry, fear of loss, and a desire to hoard, rather than to share, invest, or take calculated risks.

Examples of scarcity thinking include:

- **Fear of Failure:** "What if I lose my money?"
- **Reluctance to Invest in Yourself:** "I can't afford to spend money on learning new skills or improving my life right now."
- **Jealousy and Competition:** "If others succeed, there will be less for me."

This mentality holds many people back from achieving wealth, both financially and in other aspects of life. When you constantly feel like you must fight for scraps, your mind cannot focus on creating abundance. The rich, however, approach the world differently.

The Abundance Mindset

In contrast, the wealthy operate from a mindset of **abundance**. They believe the world is full of endless opportunities, resources, and wealth that can be created, not just taken. They understand that money, like any resource, is not finite. It can grow, expand, and regenerate when managed well.

Some examples of abundance thinking are:

- **Optimism in the Face of Risk:** "If I invest in this, it will grow, and I'll learn valuable lessons even if I fail."
- **Collaboration Over Competition:** "If I help others succeed, we'll create more opportunities for everyone."
- **Investment in Growth:** "I can always earn more money, but the knowledge and skills I acquire will stay with me forever."

When you adopt an abundant mindset, you stop fearing loss and start looking for ways to expand your world. Wealthy individuals believe that success is not a zero-sum game, where one person's win means another's loss. Instead, they see opportunities for growth everywhere.

The Importance of Optimism in Building Wealth

A key characteristic of those who become rich is **optimism**. Optimism is not about being naive or ignoring risks, but about believing in possibilities. The rich often face the same setbacks, failures, and risks as anyone else, but their optimism allows them to persevere, take calculated risks, and remain focused on their goals.

Think of optimism as the fuel for your financial journey. Without it, you run out of energy, enthusiasm, and the drive needed to overcome obstacles. The rich keep their eyes on long-term goals and believe in their ability to create solutions to any problems they encounter. Their optimism propels them to act, where others might hesitate or retreat in fear.

Consider this: if you believed there were unlimited opportunities to earn more, invest smarter, and grow faster, wouldn't you behave differently than someone who believes the world is running out of possibilities?

How to Train Your Brain to See Opportunities

One of the most powerful aspects of an abundant mindset is the ability to see opportunities where others see problems. Wealthy individuals are opportunity hunters.

They actively look for ways to create value, solve problems, and build wealth through new ventures.

Here's how you can begin training your brain to think like a rich man:

1. **Surround Yourself with Positivity:** Environment plays a huge role in shaping our thoughts. Start by surrounding yourself with people, content, and environments that reinforce the concept of abundance. Read books about success, follow entrepreneurs or thought leaders, and network with people who think big. The more you expose yourself to abundant thinking, the more it will influence your own thought patterns.

2. **Practice Gratitude**: One simple way to start cultivating an abundant mindset is through practicing gratitude. The more you focus on what you already have, the more you'll see possibilities for expansion. Wealthy people focus on what's working well in their lives and how they can build upon it, rather than dwelling on what they lack. Take time each day to reflect on the opportunities and resources already available to you.

3. **Shift from "I Can't" to "How Can I?":** When faced with challenges, train your brain to shift from negative to positive thinking. Instead of saying "I can't afford this," ask, "How can I afford this?" Instead of "There's no way I can succeed," ask, "What will it take for me to succeed?" This

shift in questioning opens your mind to solutions rather than closing it off with limiting beliefs.

4. **Visualize Success:** Rich individuals are often strong visualizers. They mentally picture their future success, envision themselves achieving their goals, and this motivates them to act. By seeing yourself as successful, wealthy, and living abundantly, you start to act in ways that align with that vision.

5. **Learn from Failures**: The road to wealth is filled with ups and downs, but those with an abundant mindset don't see failure as the end. Instead, they see it as a steppingstone to learning and growth. When something doesn't go as planned, ask yourself, "What did I learn from this?" The rich see every failure as valuable data that informs their future decisions.

Action Step: Begin Shifting Your Mindset

Take some time to reflect on your current mindset. Do you tend to think in terms of scarcity or abundance? What are some areas of your life where you can begin adopting an abundant mindset? Start small by practicing gratitude, embracing optimism, and actively seeking opportunities.

The path to wealth begins in the mind. By training your brain to think abundantly, you'll set the foundation for long-term success and prosperity.

Chapter 2: Embrace Long-Term Thinking

Delayed Gratification: A Wealthy Man's Skill

One of the most important traits that separates the wealthy from those who struggle financially is their ability to delay gratification. While many people prioritize immediate pleasure and short-term rewards, rich individuals understand the value of waiting for greater returns in the future.

What Is Delayed Gratification?

Delayed gratification is the practice of resisting the temptation of an immediate reward in favor of a more substantial one that will come later. It's about discipline, self-control, and making decisions that may not give you instant pleasure but will lead to significant gains over time.

In today's world, everything is designed for instant gratification. You can order food, buy clothes, and even get entertainment with the click of a button. The concept of waiting feels almost outdated. But the wealthy understand that true success requires patience.

Why Delayed Gratification Leads to Wealth

Here's a simple example: Imagine two people who each receive $1,000. The first person, driven by immediate desires, spends the entire amount on luxury items and experiences that provide temporary enjoyment but have no lasting value. The second person invests the $1,000 in a stock or business opportunity. Over time, that $1,000 grows into a much larger sum through compound interest or business growth.

This is how the wealthy think. They understand that money is a tool that, when used wisely, grows over time. Their focus is not on the quick win, but on the long-term game, where wealth accumulates and opportunities multiply.

Thinking in Decades, Not Days

The rich approach their goals with a long-term vision. They think not just in terms of the next month or year, but in **decades**. This long-term mindset allows them to build wealth slowly but surely, without the pressure of immediate results.

Building Wealth Slowly

Wealth doesn't happen overnight. The stories of overnight success often miss the years of hard work, risk-taking, and planning that led to that moment. Whether they are building businesses, investing in real estate, or acquiring stocks, wealthy people understand that these assets take time to mature. They are willing to sacrifice short-term gains for long-term wealth.

When you start thinking in terms of decades, you make decisions differently. For example:

- Instead of spending $500 on a gadget, you may choose to invest it in a mutual fund that will appreciate over the next 20 years.

- Rather than jumping from one job to another for a small salary increase, you might focus on building skills that will significantly raise your earning potential over the long term.

The Power of Compounding

One of the most powerful tools the rich use to their advantage is the principle of compounding. Compounding is the process where the gains on your investments earn returns, and those returns generate more returns. The longer your money is invested, the greater the effect of compounding.

For example, if you invest $1,000 at an 8% annual return, after 10 years, that money grows to approximately $2,159. But after 30 years, it grows to $10,062. The key to maximizing compounding is time. The longer you leave your money to grow, the more powerful the effect becomes.

Building Patience and Persistence for Lasting Success

Patience is a cornerstone of long-term thinking. In a world of instant gratification, patience is a superpower that the rich possess in abundance. They understand that success—whether in business, investments, or personal growth—takes time. They don't rush decisions. Instead, they plan, research, and let things develop naturally.

The Art of Staying the Course

Persistence is the ability to continue working towards a goal, even when progress is slow, or obstacles appear. Many people give up when results don't come quickly enough. The wealthy, on the other hand, understand that wealth-building requires consistent effort over time.

Let's look at a few ways you can develop this persistence:

1. **Set Long-Term Goals:** Wealthy individuals have long-term financial and personal goals. They understand that a clear vision of the future helps them stay focused. You should start by defining where you want to be in 10, 20, or 30 years. What kind of lifestyle do you want? How much wealth do you need to sustain that lifestyle? Use this as motivation to stay the course.

2. **Break Down Big Goals into Small Steps:** While long-term goals are essential, they can often seem overwhelming. The secret to achieving them is breaking them down into smaller, manageable steps. For instance, if your goal is to accumulate $1 million in assets over the next 20 years, break that goal into yearly or even monthly savings and investment targets. This way, you'll have a clear

plan to follow, and each small success will motivate you to keep going.

3. **Stay Consistent:** One of the reasons people struggle to build wealth is inconsistency. They may save for a few months, but then splurge on a luxury vacation, wiping out all their progress. Wealthy people are consistent in their approach. They develop habits that they stick to year after year, whether it's putting away a set percentage of their income for investments or continuously learning new skills to increase their value.

Why Short-Term Thinking Holds People Back

Short-term thinking often feels more comfortable. It gives us quick results, immediate satisfaction, and a sense of progress. However, this type of thinking can significantly hinder your financial success in the long run.

Focusing on Instant Wins

Many people focus on short-term rewards like buying a new car, the latest smartphone, or expensive dinners. While these purchases might make you feel successful temporarily, they don't contribute to long-term financial growth. The problem with short-term thinking is that it usually prioritizes consumption over creation, preventing you from building assets that will serve you in the future.

The Debt Trap

Short-term thinking also leads many into the trap of debt. Credit cards and loans make it easy to buy things you can't afford right now, but the cost of that convenience can be high. High-interest rates on loans and credit cards can quickly accumulate, reducing your financial freedom. Wealthy individuals avoid unnecessary debt, especially when it's used to finance short-term desires rather than long-term investments.

Lack of Planning

When you think only in the short term, you may lack the foresight needed to plan. Whether it's saving for retirement, creating an emergency fund, or investing in assets that appreciate over time, short-term thinking makes it difficult to prepare for life's larger challenges and opportunities.

How to Develop a Long-Term Perspective

Building a long-term perspective takes practice, but once you master it, you'll begin to make better decisions that will lead to lasting wealth and success. Here are a few ways to start:

1. **Focus on Big Picture Goals:** Spend time defining your big picture—what you want your financial future to look like. Start with your retirement goals, investment plans, and lifestyle aspirations. When you keep the bigger picture in mind, it

becomes easier to make decisions that align with your long-term objectives.

2. **Reward Yourself Strategically**: While long-term thinking is critical, it's also important to reward yourself along the way. The key is to do it in a strategic manner. For instance, you could treat yourself to something small after hitting a major savings milestone, rather than indulging impulsively. This helps you enjoy the journey without sacrificing your long-term vision.

3. **Visualize Your Future Success**: Visualizing your long-term success can be a powerful motivator. Picture yourself living the life you've worked so hard to create—a life of financial freedom, comfort, and fulfillment. Visualization can reinforce the importance of making sacrifices today for a better tomorrow.

4. **Track Your Progress**: One way to stay motivated with long-term thinking is by tracking your progress. Whether it's through an investment account, savings goal, or personal development milestones, seeing how far you've come can keep you focused and persistent.

Action Step: Start Thinking Long-Term

Take time today to reflect on your long-term goals. Write down where you want to be financially and personally in

5, 10, or 20 years. Next, identify a few small steps you can take to get there. This might include setting up an investment account, learning a new skill, or creating a budget that prioritizes long-term savings.

Remember, the journey to wealth is a marathon, not a sprint. Long-term thinking is the key to sustained success.

Chapter 3: Confidence and Self-Worth

Believing in Yourself as an Investment

Confidence is often seen as a byproduct of success, but it is the foundation upon which success is built. The rich understand that to achieve wealth, they first need to believe in their own value, capabilities, and potential. Self-confidence isn't just a trait; it's a strategy. It influences how you take risks, seize opportunities, and approach challenges.

When you think of yourself as an asset, everything changes. Just like how a wealthy individual sees their money as something to be invested and grown, they view themselves the same way. They invest in their skills, health, and relationships, knowing that the returns on these investments will compound over time.

Why Confidence Matters for Wealth Building

Here's how confidence plays a critical role in financial success:

- **Confidence Encourages Risk-Taking:** Those with strong self-belief are more likely to take calculated risks. Whether it's investing in a business, taking on a leadership role, or negotiating for higher pay, confidence drives action. Wealthy individuals understand that success often requires stepping into the unknown and believing in their ability to adapt and succeed.

- **Confidence Attracts Opportunities:** When you exude confidence, people are more likely to trust and engage with you. This opens doors to new opportunities, partnerships, and collaborations. Whether in business or social settings, confidence is magnetic. Wealthy people know how to project self-assurance, which in turn draws others toward them.

- **Confidence Breeds Resilience:** Financial success is often a journey filled with setbacks and challenges. Confidence gives you the resilience to keep moving forward, even when things don't go as planned. Wealthy individuals believe in their ability to recover from failure, learn from mistakes, and grow stronger.

How to Build Unshakeable Confidence

If confidence is the foundation of success, how do you develop it, especially if it doesn't come naturally? The good news is that confidence is a skill, and like any skill, it can be cultivated. The wealthy understand that confidence is not something you're born with, but something you build over time.

Here are strategies that can help you build unshakeable confidence:

1. **Invest in Knowledge and Skills**: One of the best ways to boost your confidence is by becoming knowledgeable and skilled in your field. The more you know, the more confident you'll feel about your decisions. Wealthy individuals are constantly learning, whether through formal education, reading, or hands-on experience. When you're informed, you feel empowered to make bold moves, take risks, and engage with others on a higher level.

2. **Set and Achieve Small Goals**: Confidence grows through small wins. Start by setting achievable goals that push you out of your comfort zone but are within reach. Each time you accomplish something, no matter how small, you reinforce the belief that you are capable of success. Over time, these small victories build into a solid foundation of confidence that will allow you to tackle bigger challenges.

3. **Embrace Failure as Part of the Process**: Many people fear failure, but wealthy individuals view failure as a necessary part of success. They don't allow mistakes to shake their confidence. Instead, they see them as learning opportunities. The key to building confidence is not avoiding failure but learning how to recover from it and move forward with more wisdom and experience.

4. **Cultivate a Growth Mindset**: A growth mindset is the belief that your abilities and intelligence can be developed through effort, learning, and persistence. This mindset helps you see challenges as opportunities for growth rather than threats to your self-worth. Wealthy individuals thrive on growth and see every obstacle as a chance to improve and adapt.

5. **Visualize Success**: Many wealthy individuals practice visualization as a tool to build confidence. They regularly picture themselves succeeding—whether it's closing a deal, running a successful business, or reaching their financial goals. Visualization helps you mentally prepare for success and reinforces your belief in your ability to achieve it. When you consistently imagine success, you are more likely to act with the confidence needed to make it a reality.

The Role of Self-Worth in Financial Success

While confidence is the outward expression of belief in yourself, self-worth is the internal understanding of your value. How you perceive your own worth directly influences how you engage with the world, especially in financial matters. The rich know that self-worth and wealth are deeply intertwined.

Self-Worth Drives Your Earning Potential

If you don't believe you are worth a high salary, you're unlikely to ask for one. If you don't believe your time is valuable, you may allow others to take advantage of it. Wealthy individuals understand their value and are not afraid to demand compensation that reflects it.

For example, a rich person sees their time as a limited, high-value resource. They charge accordingly for their services or expertise and are selective about how they spend their time. This level of self-worth is crucial to growing wealth, as it sets the tone for how you expect to be treated and compensated in all areas of life.

Avoid Undervaluing Yourself

Many people struggle financially because they undervalue themselves. They accept jobs that pay less than they deserve, don't negotiate salaries, or allow others to dictate their financial worth. Wealthy people, on the other hand, know that they bring value to the table and are not afraid to negotiate or walk away from deals that don't honor their worth.

If you constantly accept less than what you deserve, whether in business or personal life, you will find it difficult to build wealth. You must believe in your inherent value to command the compensation and respect you desire.

How to Increase Your Self-Worth

Developing a strong sense of self-worth is a gradual process, but it's essential for anyone looking to behave like a rich person. Here are some strategies to help you enhance your self-worth:

1. **Set Boundaries and Respect Your Time**: Wealthy individuals are highly protective of their time. They don't allow others to waste it or exploit it. Start by setting clear boundaries for how others treat you, both personally and professionally. If you value your time, others will begin to respect it as well. Be willing to say no to opportunities that don't align with your goals or don't offer the right compensation for your value.

2. **Stop Comparing Yourself to Others**: Many people diminish their self-worth by constantly comparing themselves to others, whether it's in terms of income, status, or material possessions. The rich understand that everyone's journey is different. Focus on your own path to success and recognize the unique value you bring to the table, rather than measuring yourself against others.

3. **Reward Yourself for Accomplishments**: Celebrating your successes, no matter how small, is an important part of building self-worth. Wealthy individuals take time to acknowledge their achievements, which reinforces their sense of accomplishment and worthiness. Make it a habit to reward yourself when you hit significant

milestones. This will build your confidence and remind you of your growing value.

4. **Invest in Your Personal Growth**: Personal growth and self-improvement are directly tied to self-worth. Wealthy individuals continuously invest in themselves, whether it's through education, personal development, or cultivating new skills. The more you grow and expand your capabilities, the more you will recognize your own value and the higher you will set your standards.

5. **Surround Yourself with People Who Uplift You**: Your environment plays a significant role in how you see yourself. Surround yourself with people who uplift and support you, rather than those who bring negativity or doubt into your life. Wealthy people often surround themselves with other high achievers who inspire them and help reinforce their self-worth. Make a conscious effort to build relationships that help you grow and see your own value.

The Wealthy Approach to Negotiation

One of the areas where confidence and self-worth show up most clearly is in negotiation. Whether it's negotiating a salary, a business deal, or even personal agreements, the wealthy approach these situations with the belief that they deserve the best possible outcome.

Here's how the rich approach negotiation:

- **They Know Their Value:** Wealthy individuals enter negotiations with a strong understanding of their own value. They know what they bring to the table and are not afraid to demand compensation that reflects that worth.

- **They Don't Settle:** Rich people don't accept the first offer if it doesn't meet their expectations. They are willing to walk away from deals that don't align with their goals or undercut their value. This mindset ensures that they are only involved in situations that enhance their wealth and success.

- **They Prepare Thoroughly:** Confidence in negotiation often comes from thorough preparation. The wealthy spend time researching, understanding market value, and preparing their arguments before entering any negotiation. This level of preparation allows them to negotiate from a position of strength.

Action Step: Build Your Confidence and Self-Worth

This week, take steps to actively build your confidence and self-worth. Identify one area where you feel undervalued, whether in your career, relationships, or personal goals. Ask yourself: What would a wealthy, confident person do in this situation? Then, act. It might mean negotiating for a raise, setting new boundaries, or investing in a skill that enhances your value. The key is to start believing in yourself as the most valuable investment in your wealth-building journey.

Chapter 4: Daily Habits of the Wealthy

The Power of Routine

Daily habits play a crucial role in the lives of wealthy individuals. While many people might expect the rich to engage in extravagant lifestyles, the truth is that consistent, disciplined routines often define their success. Routines create structure and provide the foundation for sustained achievement over time.

Why Habits Matter

Habits are the small decisions you make and actions you take every day. They can lead to extraordinary results. Research suggests that about 40% of our daily actions are habitual, meaning that many of the things we do are automatic and often subconscious. By cultivating productive habits, the wealthy maximize their time and energy, leading to more significant outcomes.

The wealthy understand that every successful action—no matter how small—accumulates over time. For them, these habits aren't just about achieving wealth; they are about creating a lifestyle of success that reinforces their goals and values.

Key Habits of the Wealthy

Here are some of the daily habits that wealthy individuals practice to build and maintain their financial success:

1. **Early Rising**: Many wealthy people start their day early, often before the rest of the world wakes up. Rising early provides a quiet time to focus, plan, and prepare for the day ahead. This habit allows them to get a jump start on their tasks, engage in self-care, and reflect on their goals.

    - **Action Tip:** Try waking up 30 minutes earlier than usual. Use this time for activities that enrich your mind and body, such as meditation, reading, or planning your day.

2. **Consistent Learning**: The rich are lifelong learners. They understand the importance of keeping their minds sharp and staying informed about their industries. Many wealthy individuals dedicate time each day to read books, listen to podcasts, or take courses that contribute to their personal and professional development.

    - **Action Tip:** Set aside at least 30 minutes a day for reading or engaging with educational content. Choose topics that interest you or relate to your field of work.

3. **Setting Clear Goals**: Successful individuals are goal oriented. They don't just have vague aspirations; they set specific, measurable goals.

Wealthy people often review their goals daily, ensuring they stay on track and adjust when necessary.

- **Action Tip:** Write down your short-term and long-term financial goals. Review them each morning to remind yourself of what you're working towards.

4. **Budgeting and Financial Tracking**: The wealthy are disciplined about their finances. They create budgets and track their expenses, ensuring they live within their means and save for the future. They understand the importance of knowing where their money is going and actively managing their finances.

    - **Action Tip:** Start tracking your spending using budgeting apps or spreadsheets. Set monthly limits for different categories and hold yourself accountable.

5. **Networking and Relationship Building**: Building and maintaining relationships is a critical habit for the wealthy. They understand that success often comes from the people they know. Wealthy individuals regularly engage in networking, attending events, and nurturing professional relationships.

    - **Action Tip:** Make it a point to connect with someone new each week, whether through social media or in-person events. Building a strong network can open doors to opportunities you may not have considered.

6. **Exercise and Well-Being**: Health is a priority for wealthy individuals. Many engage in regular exercise, whether through gym workouts, outdoor activities, or sports. Physical well-being fuels their energy and enhances their productivity.
   - **Action Tip:** Incorporate physical activity into your daily routine, whether it's a morning workout, a walk during lunch, or evening yoga. Prioritize your health to enhance your overall performance.

Developing Discipline Through Consistency

Discipline is about making choices that align with your long-term goals, even when it's challenging. Wealthy individuals cultivate discipline through consistent practice of their daily habits. Here's how you can develop discipline in your own life:

1. **Create a Structured Schedule**: Establishing a structured daily schedule helps you stay organized and focused. Allocate specific time slots for work, learning, exercise, and relaxation. A clear schedule reduces decision fatigue and keeps you on track.

2. **Start Small and Build Up**: If you're trying to adopt new habits, start small. For instance, instead of committing to a full hour of exercise each day, start with 10-15 minutes. As you become comfortable, gradually increase the duration. Small successes build confidence and pave the way for larger changes.

3. **Eliminate Distractions**: Identify distractions in your environment that hinder your productivity. Whether it's social media, excessive notifications, or a cluttered workspace, take steps to minimize these interruptions. Create a dedicated space for work and learning where you can focus without distractions.

4. **Hold Yourself Accountable**: Accountability is a powerful motivator. Share your goals with someone you trust or consider joining a group or community with similar objectives. Regular check-ins with a mentor or accountability partner can keep you motivated and committed to your daily habits.

5. **Celebrate Your Progress**: Acknowledge and celebrate your accomplishments, no matter how small. Recognizing your achievements reinforces positive behavior and motivates you to keep going. Consider rewarding yourself for reaching milestones, which can reinforce your discipline.

Building Wealth through Small Daily Actions

The small actions you take each day can lead to significant financial gains over time. Wealthy individuals understand that consistent, disciplined actions—like saving a portion of their income or investing regularly—compound to create wealth.

The Importance of Compound Growth

Just as money grows through compound interest, your daily habits compound over time. For example, if you save just $10 a day and invest it at a 5% annual return, you'll have over $18,000 in 20 years. This principle applies not only to finances but also to skills, knowledge, and personal development.

The Wealthy Mindset: Abundance vs. Scarcity

Another daily habit of the wealthy is cultivating an abundance mindset. They focus on opportunities rather than limitations. This mindset shapes their actions and decisions, enabling them to see potential where others may only see challenges.

- **Embracing Opportunities**: Wealthy individuals actively seek out opportunities for growth and investment. They see potential in situations that others might overlook. An abundance mindset allows them to take calculated risks, leading to increased financial success.

- **Overcoming Fear of Failure**: The wealthy understand that failure is a part of the journey to success. Rather than fearing it, they embrace it as a learning experience. This perspective encourages them to take bold actions, knowing that every setback can lead to future growth.

Action Step: Evaluate Your Daily Habits

Take a moment to assess your daily routines. Identify one or two habits that you can implement this week to move toward your financial goals. Consider what successful people do and incorporate those practices into your life.

Chapter 5: Financial Literacy and Money Management

Understanding Financial Literacy

Financial literacy is the foundation of wealth-building. It encompasses the knowledge and skills necessary to make informed and effective decisions regarding money management. Wealthy individuals prioritize financial literacy as a critical element of their success, allowing them to navigate the complex world of finance confidently.

Why Financial Literacy Matters

A lack of financial literacy can lead to poor decision-making, missed opportunities, and financial instability. Here are a few reasons why it's essential:

- **Informed Decision-Making:** Understanding financial concepts allows you to evaluate investment opportunities, choose suitable savings plans, and make sound financial decisions.
- **Risk Management:** Knowledge of financial principles helps you assess risks, whether in investing, taking out loans, or starting a business. This awareness enables you to make choices that align with your risk tolerance and financial goals.

- **Wealth Accumulation:** The wealthy are adept at using their financial knowledge to grow their wealth. They understand concepts such as compound interest, investment diversification, and tax strategies, which allow them to maximize their financial potential.

Key Components of Financial Literacy

To build your financial literacy, focus on mastering these key components:

1. **Understanding Basic Financial Concepts:** Familiarize yourself with fundamental financial terms and concepts, such as:
    - **Income:** Money received from work, investments, or other sources.
    - **Expenses:** Costs incurred while living and doing business.
    - **Savings:** Funds set aside for future use.
    - **Investments:** Assets purchased with the expectation of generating returns.
    - **Credit:** Borrowed money that must be repaid, often with interest.
    - **Action Tip:** Create flashcards for essential financial terms and concepts to reinforce your understanding.

2. **Budgeting Skills**: Effective budgeting is crucial for financial stability. A budget allows you to track income and expenses, prioritize spending, and identify areas for saving. Wealthy individuals typically allocate a portion of their income to savings and investments, ensuring they build wealth over time.

    - **Action Tip:** Use budgeting apps or spreadsheets to track your monthly income and expenses. Aim to create a budget that includes a savings component.

3. **Investment Knowledge**: Understanding different types of investments, such as stocks, bonds, real estate, and mutual funds, is vital for wealth building. Wealthy individuals often have diversified portfolios that balance risk and return, ensuring their money works for them.

    - **Action Tip:** Take the time to research different investment vehicles and their potential risks and rewards. Consider opening a brokerage account to start investing with small amounts.

4. **Debt Management**: The wealthy know how to manage debt effectively. They understand the difference between good debt (which can help you build wealth) and bad debt (which can hinder financial growth). Developing strategies to pay

down high-interest debt while leveraging low-interest debt for investments is a critical skill.

- o **Action Tip:** Create a plan to pay off any high-interest debt first, such as credit card balances. Consider consolidating loans or negotiating lower interest rates when possible.

5. **Understanding Taxes**: Knowledge of tax laws and strategies can significantly impact your financial success. Wealthy individuals often work with financial advisors to minimize their tax liabilities, using legal deductions and credits to keep more of their income.

    - o **Action Tip:** Learn about tax deductions that may apply to you and consider consulting a tax professional for personalized advice.

Building a Strong Money Management Strategy

Once you have a foundation of financial literacy, it's essential to develop a robust money management strategy. Here are steps to guide you:

1. **Create a Financial Plan**: A comprehensive financial plan outlines your financial goals, income, expenses, and investment strategies. This plan serves as a roadmap to guide your financial

decisions and keep you on track toward achieving your objectives.

- **Action Tip:** Write down your short-term and long-term financial goals. Include specifics, such as how much money you want to save or invest in the next five years.

2. **Establish an Emergency Fund**: An emergency fund acts as a safety net during unexpected financial challenges. Wealthy individuals typically maintain several months' worth of living expenses in liquid assets to ensure they can weather financial storms.

   - **Action Tip:** Aim to save three to six months' worth of expenses in a high-yield savings account. Start small and gradually build your fund over time.

3. **Invest Regularly**: Consistent investing is crucial for building wealth. Wealthy individuals often contribute to retirement accounts and investment portfolios regularly. This habit allows them to take advantage of market fluctuations and compound interest.

   - **Action Tip:** Set up automatic contributions to your investment accounts to ensure you consistently invest a portion of your income.

4. **Review and Adjust Your Financial Plan**: Regularly reviewing your financial plan ensures that you stay on track toward your goals. Wealthy individuals frequently reassess their financial situation, adjusting based on changes in income, expenses, and market conditions.

    o **Action Tip:** Schedule time each quarter to review your budget, expenses, and investments. Make necessary adjustments to stay aligned with your financial goals.

The Role of Advisors and Mentors

Many wealthy individuals seek guidance from financial advisors, accountants, and mentors. These professionals can provide valuable insights, strategies, and support, helping you make informed decisions.

- **Financial Advisors:** They can help you create a comprehensive financial plan, manage investments, and optimize your tax strategies. Finding a trustworthy advisor can greatly enhance your financial journey.

- **Mentors:** Connecting with experienced individuals in your field can provide valuable knowledge and support. Wealthy people often surround themselves with mentors who can guide them through challenges and help them seize opportunities.

Action Step: Assess Your Financial Literacy

Take a moment to evaluate your current level of financial literacy. Identify areas where you feel confident and those where you need improvement. Create a plan to enhance your knowledge in those areas, whether through online courses, reading, or seeking mentorship.

Chapter 6: The Mindset of Wealth and Abundance

The Power of Mindset

Your mindset shapes how you view the world and approach life's challenges. For wealthy individuals, a positive and growth-oriented mindset is crucial for achieving and maintaining financial success. Understanding the difference between a scarcity mindset and an abundance mindset can help you cultivate the thoughts and beliefs that lead to wealth.

Scarcity vs. Abundance Mindset

- **Scarcity Mindset:** Individuals with a scarcity mindset often believe that resources are limited. They may feel that there is never enough money, time, or opportunity to go around. This mindset can lead to fear, anxiety, and poor financial decisions, such as hoarding money or avoiding investments.

- **Abundance Mindset:** Conversely, those with an abundance mindset believe that opportunities and resources are plentiful. They view challenges as opportunities for growth and are more likely to take calculated risks. This mindset encourages generosity, creativity, and the pursuit of new possibilities.

Wealthy individuals cultivate an abundance mindset, which allows them to embrace opportunities and foster growth in their financial lives.

Cultivating an Abundance Mindset

To develop an abundance mindset, consider implementing the following strategies:

1. **Practice Gratitude**: Gratitude is a powerful tool for shifting your perspective. Regularly acknowledging and appreciating what you have fosters a sense of abundance. Wealthy individuals often practice gratitude to maintain a positive outlook and attract more good things into their lives.

    - **Action Tip:** Keep a gratitude journal and write down three things you are grateful for each day. Reflect on how these positives contribute to your overall well-being.

2. **Challenge Limiting Beliefs**: Many people harbor limiting beliefs about money, such as "I'll never be wealthy" or "Money is the root of all evil." Identify and challenge these beliefs. Replace them with empowering affirmations that support your goals, such as "I am capable of creating wealth" or "Opportunities for success are everywhere."

- **Action Tip:** Create a list of limiting beliefs you hold about money and reframe them into positive affirmations. Repeat these affirmations daily to reinforce a more empowering mindset.

3. **Surround Yourself with Positivity**: The people you spend time with can significantly influence your mindset. Surrounding yourself with individuals who have an abundance mindset can inspire and motivate you to adopt similar beliefs and behaviors. Wealthy individuals often network with like-minded people who uplift and encourage their aspirations.
   - **Action Tip:** Seek out mentors, friends, and communities that foster a positive and growth-oriented environment. Engage in discussions about success, wealth, and opportunities.

4. **Invest in Personal Development**: Committing to lifelong learning and personal development is a hallmark of wealthy individuals. They view challenges as opportunities to grow and learn. Investing in your skills and knowledge can boost your confidence and expand your horizons.
   - **Action Tip:** Take a course, attend workshops, or read books on personal development, finance, and wealth-

building. Focus on topics that resonate with your goals and aspirations.

Embracing Risk and Failure

An abundance mindset encourages individuals to embrace risk and view failure as a learning experience. Wealthy individuals understand that taking calculated risks is often necessary for growth and success. Here's how to shift your perspective on risk and failure:

1. **Reframe Failure**: Rather than viewing failure as a setback, see it as an opportunity for growth. Each failure can teach valuable lessons that propel you closer to your goals. Wealthy individuals often analyze their failures, extract lessons, and apply those insights to future endeavors.

    - **Action Tip:** After experiencing a setback, take time to reflect on what went wrong and what you can learn from the experience. Write down your insights and use them to inform your future actions.

2. **Take Calculated Risks**: Risk is inherent in any pursuit of success. Wealthy individuals evaluate potential risks and rewards, making informed decisions about where to invest their time, energy, and resources. They understand that calculated risks can lead to significant rewards.

- **Action Tip:** When considering a new opportunity or investment, conduct thorough research and weigh the potential risks against the benefits. Make informed decisions based on your analysis.

Visualization and Goal Setting

Wealthy individuals often practice visualization techniques to reinforce their goals and maintain a positive mindset. Visualizing success helps create a mental image of your desired outcomes, making them feel more attainable. Here's how to incorporate visualization into your routine:

1. **Create a Vision Board**: A vision board is a visual representation of your goals and aspirations. It serves as a constant reminder of what you want to achieve. Include images, quotes, and affirmations that inspire you and align with your financial objectives.

    - **Action Tip:** Spend time creating a vision board that represents your financial and personal goals. Place it in a visible location where you will see it daily.

2. **Practice Daily Visualization**: Take a few moments each day to visualize yourself achieving your goals. Imagine the feelings, experiences, and success associated with reaching those milestones.

This practice reinforces your commitment to your aspirations and attracts positive energy toward them.

- **Action Tip:** Find a quiet space where you can practice visualization for 5-10 minutes each day. Focus on your goals and the emotions associated with achieving them.

Action Step: Assess Your Mindset

Take time to reflect on your current mindset regarding wealth and abundance. Ask yourself:

- Do I have a scarcity or abundance mindset?
- What limiting beliefs do I hold about money?
- How can I cultivate a more positive and abundant mindset?

Identify one or two specific actions you can take this week to shift your mindset toward abundance.

Chapter 7: Networking and Building Wealthy Relationships

The Power of Networking

Networking is often cited as one of the most crucial elements in the journey toward financial success. Building relationships with like-minded individuals and influential contacts can create opportunities for collaboration, mentorship, and investment. Wealthy individuals understand that their network is one of their most valuable assets.

Why Networking Matters

- **Opportunities:** Networking can open doors to job offers, partnerships, and investment opportunities that might not be available through traditional channels.

- **Support and Guidance:** A strong network provides access to mentors who can offer advice, share experiences, and guide you through challenges. Learning from others who have achieved financial success can help you navigate your own path more effectively.

- **Collaboration:** Many wealthy individuals collaborate with others to create businesses, share resources, or invest in ventures. Building relationships fosters a spirit of collaboration and innovation.

Strategies for Effective Networking

To cultivate a powerful network, consider the following strategies:

1. **Identify Your Goals**: Before you begin networking, clarify your goals. What do you hope to achieve? Are you looking for mentorship, investment opportunities, or partnerships? Understanding your objectives will help you identify the right individuals to connect with.

    - **Action Tip:** Write down your networking goals. Specify the types of relationships you want to build and how they align with your financial aspirations.

2. **Attend Networking Events**: Attend industry conferences, seminars, workshops, and social events where you can meet potential contacts. Many wealthy individuals invest time in networking events to expand their circles and meet influential people.

    - **Action Tip:** Research upcoming events in your industry or area of interest. Make it a goal to attend at least one event each month.

3. **Leverage social media**: Platforms like LinkedIn, Twitter, and Facebook can be powerful tools for networking. Use these platforms to connect with industry leaders, engage in discussions, and share valuable content. Regularly post updates about your own experiences and achievements to attract attention.

    - **Action Tip:** Optimize your social media profiles to reflect your professional goals. Start reaching out to people in your network with whom you'd like to connect or collaborate.

4. **Be Genuine and Authentic**: Building meaningful relationships requires authenticity. Wealthy individuals prioritize genuine connections over superficial interactions. Show genuine interest in others, ask questions, and listen actively.

    - **Action Tip:** When networking, focus on building relationships rather than just exchanging business cards. Follow up with new contacts after events to continue the conversation.

5. **Follow Up**: After meeting someone new, be sure to follow up with a personalized message. This gesture reinforces your interest in building a relationship and helps you stay top of mind. Include a specific reference to your conversation to make your follow-up more personal.

- **Action Tip:** Create a system for tracking new contacts and follow up within 48 hours of meeting someone. Use notes to remember key details from your conversation.

Building Wealthy Relationships

Beyond networking, nurturing relationships is essential for long-term success. Here are some strategies for fostering meaningful connections:

1. **Offer Value**: Building relationships is a two-way street. Consider how you can provide value to others in your network. Whether it's sharing resources, offering support, or providing introductions, contributing to others' success fosters goodwill and strengthens bonds.
   - **Action Tip:** Identify one way you can support someone in your network this week. It could be sharing an article, making an introduction, or helping with a project.

2. **Seek Mentorship**: Finding a mentor can significantly accelerate your journey to financial success. A mentor can provide invaluable insights, guidance, and accountability. Wealthy individuals often attribute their success to the guidance they received from mentors.

- **Action Tip:** Identify potential mentors in your network or industry. Reach out to them with a respectful request for guidance or advice. Be specific about what you hope to learn.

3. **Join Professional Organizations**: Becoming a member of professional associations or groups related to your industry can expand your network and provide access to exclusive resources. Many wealthy individuals actively participate in such organizations to connect with peers and industry leaders.

    - **Action Tip:** Research professional organizations in your field and consider joining. Attend their events and engage with fellow members.

4. **Stay in Touch**: Regularly check in with your contacts, even when you don't need anything. Sending a quick message or sharing relevant articles can keep your relationships alive and show that you value their connection.

    - **Action Tip:** Schedule regular reminders to reach out to contacts in your network. Aim to connect with at least one person each week.

Networking Mindset: Be Open to Opportunities

Wealthy individuals maintain a networking mindset that is open to possibilities. They understand that opportunities can arise from unexpected connections and conversations. Here are ways to cultivate an open mindset:

1. **Be Curious**: Approach networking with curiosity. Ask questions, seek to understand others' experiences, and explore how your goals align with theirs. Curiosity fosters connection and allows you to discover potential collaborations.

    o **Action Tip:** Practice active listening during conversations. Focus on understanding others' perspectives rather than planning your response.

2. **Embrace Diversity**: Building a diverse network enhances your perspectives and opportunities. Connect with people from different backgrounds, industries, and experiences. Diverse networks can lead to innovative ideas and collaborations.

    o **Action Tip:** Make a conscious effort to connect with individuals outside your usual circles. Attend events or forums that attract diverse participants.

Action Step: Evaluate Your Network

Take time to assess your current network. Ask yourself:

- Who are the key contacts in your network?
- How can I strengthen these relationships?
- Are there individuals I would like to connect with but haven't yet?

Identify at least one specific action you can take this week to expand or strengthen your network.

Chapter 8: Investment Strategies for Wealth Building

Understanding Investment Basics

Investing is a powerful tool for building wealth and achieving financial independence. While saving is essential for short-term financial stability, investing allows your money to grow over time, often outpacing inflation and increasing your purchasing power. Wealthy individuals often view investments as a crucial component of their financial strategy.

Key Investment Concepts

- **Risk and Return:** Generally, higher potential returns come with higher risks. Understanding your risk tolerance is essential for creating an investment strategy that aligns with your financial goals.

- **Diversification:** Spreading your investments across various asset classes (stocks, bonds, real estate, etc.) helps mitigate risk. Wealthy individuals often maintain diversified portfolios to protect their wealth.

- **Time Horizon:** Your investment time horizon—the length of time you plan to hold an investment—affects your strategy. Longer time horizons can afford to take on more risk, as there is more time to recover from market fluctuations.

Types of Investments

There are several types of investments, each with unique characteristics, risks, and potential returns:

1. **Stocks**: Investing in stocks involves buying shares of ownership in a company. Stocks can provide substantial returns but come with higher risks due to market volatility.
    - **Growth Stocks:** Companies expected to grow at an above-average rate compared to their industry. They typically do not pay dividends, as profits are reinvested for expansion.
    - **Dividend Stocks:** Companies that pay regular dividends to shareholders. These can provide income and potential for capital appreciation.
    - **Action Tip:** Research stocks in industries you are interested in and consider starting with small investments to build your understanding.
2. **Bonds**: Bonds are fixed-income investments where you loan money to a company or government in exchange for periodic interest

payments and the return of the bond's face value at maturity. They are generally considered lower risk than stocks.

- **Corporate Bonds:** Issued by companies and can offer higher yields than government bonds.
- **Municipal Bonds:** Issued by local governments and often tax-exempt, making them attractive for certain investors.
- **Action Tip:** Consider incorporating bonds into your portfolio to balance the risk associated with stocks.

3. **Real Estate**: Real estate can provide both rental income and potential for appreciation. Wealthy individuals often invest in properties to generate passive income and diversify their portfolios.

    - **Residential Real Estate:** Investing in rental properties, such as single-family homes or multi-family units.
    - **Commercial Real Estate:** Investing in office buildings, retail spaces, or industrial properties.
    - **Action Tip:** Explore local real estate markets and consider options for investing,

whether through direct ownership or real estate investment trusts (REITs).

4. **Mutual Funds and ETFs**: Mutual funds and exchange-traded funds (ETFs) pool money from multiple investors to buy a diversified portfolio of stocks or bonds. They offer a simple way to diversify without having to manage individual investments.

    - **Mutual Funds:** Professionally managed and can be actively or passively managed. They typically have higher fees.

    - **ETFs:** Trade like stocks and often have lower fees. They can provide exposure to various sectors or markets.

    - **Action Tip:** Research and compare mutual funds and ETFs that align with your investment goals and risk tolerance.

Building an Investment Strategy

Developing a solid investment strategy is essential for long-term success. Consider these steps:

1. **Set Clear Financial Goals**: Establish your investment objectives, such as saving for retirement, buying a home, or funding education. Clear goals provide direction and help you measure your progress.

- **Action Tip:** Write down your financial goals, specifying timelines and target amounts.

2. **Assess Your Risk Tolerance**: Understand your comfort level with risk. Factors influencing your risk tolerance include your age, financial situation, investment goals, and experience.
    - **Action Tip:** Take a risk tolerance questionnaire online to evaluate your comfort level with various investment scenarios.

3. **Create a Diversified Portfolio**: Construct a diversified portfolio that reflects your risk tolerance and investment goals. Include a mix of asset classes, such as stocks, bonds, and real estate, to balance risk and potential returns.
    - **Action Tip:** Use investment apps or tools to help you design a diversified portfolio based on your financial profile.

4. **Regularly Review and Rebalance Your Portfolio**: Over time, your portfolio may drift away from your target allocation due to market fluctuations. Regularly reviewing and rebalancing your portfolio ensures that it remains aligned with your goals.
    - **Action Tip:** Schedule regular portfolio reviews (e.g., quarterly or annually) to

assess performance and make necessary adjustments.

Investing for the Long Term

Wealthy individuals often adopt a long-term investment strategy, understanding that building wealth takes time. Here are some principles for successful long-term investing:

1. **Stay Committed**: Investing can be volatile, and market fluctuations are inevitable. Stay committed to your long-term strategy and avoid making impulsive decisions based on short-term market movements.
    - **Action Tip:** Develop a plan for how you will respond to market downturns. Consider automatic contributions to your investment accounts during market dips.

2. **Harness the Power of Compound Interest**: Investing early and consistently allows you to benefit from compound interest, where your investment earnings generate additional earnings over time. This can significantly amplify your wealth.
    - **Action Tip:** Start investing as soon as possible, even if it's a small amount. The

sooner you begin, the more time your money must grow.

3. **Continuous Learning**: Stay informed about investment trends, market conditions, and financial strategies. Wealthy individuals prioritize ongoing education to adapt their strategies and seize new opportunities.
    - **Action Tip:** Dedicate time each month to read financial news, books, or take courses related to investing and personal finance.

Action Step: Develop Your Investment Plan

Take a moment to outline your investment plan. Consider:

- What are your financial goals, and what timeline do you have for achieving them?
- What is your risk tolerance, and how will it influence your investment choices?
- What types of investments do you want to include in your portfolio?

Create a plan that outlines your investment objectives and steps to achieve them.

Chapter 9: Personal Branding and Marketing Yourself for Success

The Importance of Personal Branding

In a world saturated with information and options, personal branding has become more critical than ever. Your personal brand is the perception others have of you based on your reputation, skills, experiences, and values. Wealthy individuals often recognize the power of personal branding in creating opportunities and building influence.

Why Personal Branding Matters

- **Differentiation:** A strong personal brand sets you apart from others in your field. It helps you highlight your unique skills and qualities that make you valuable in the marketplace.

- **Credibility and Trust:** Establishing a solid personal brand fosters credibility and trust. People are more likely to engage with and invest in individuals they perceive as trustworthy and knowledgeable.

- **Opportunities for Collaboration:** A strong personal brand attracts opportunities for collaboration, partnerships, and mentorship. When people recognize your expertise, they are more likely to seek you out for potential ventures.

Building Your Personal Brand

To develop a compelling personal brand, consider the following steps:

1. **Define Your Brand Identity**: Begin by identifying your values, passions, and unique skills. Understanding what you stand for and what makes you unique is the foundation of your personal brand.

    - **Action Tip:** Write a personal mission statement that summarizes your values and what you want to achieve in your career. This statement will guide your branding efforts.

2. **Create an Online Presence**: In today's digital age, having an online presence is crucial for personal branding. Utilize platforms such as LinkedIn, personal websites, and social media to showcase your expertise and connect with your audience.

    - **Action Tip:** Optimize your LinkedIn profile with a professional photo, detailed work experience, and a summary that reflects your personal brand. Consider starting a blog or a website to share your insights and expertise.

3. **Consistent Messaging**: Ensure your messaging is consistent across all platforms. Your tone, visuals, and content should reflect your personal brand and resonate with your target audience.
   - **Action Tip:** Create a style guide for your personal brand that outlines your preferred tone, color scheme, and content themes. Use this guide to maintain consistency in your messaging.

4. **Network and Engage**: Building a personal brand involves actively engaging with your audience and industry peers. Participate in discussions, share valuable content, and connect with others in your field.
   - **Action Tip:** Dedicate time each week to engage with your network on social media. Comment on posts, share articles, and participate in relevant discussions.

Marketing Yourself Effectively

Once you have established your personal brand, it's time to market yourself effectively. Here are some strategies to consider:

1. **Leverage Social Proof**: Social proof, such as testimonials, endorsements, and case studies, can enhance your credibility and attract opportunities.

Highlighting positive feedback from others reinforces your expertise.

- **Action Tip:** Reach out to colleagues, mentors, or clients for testimonials that showcase your skills and achievements. Display these testimonials prominently on your online profiles.

2. **Content Creation**: Creating valuable content, such as articles, videos, or podcasts, positions you as an authority in your field. Sharing your knowledge and insights not only builds your brand but also attracts followers and potential opportunities.

    - **Action Tip:** Start a blog or a YouTube channel where you can share your expertise. Aim to post regularly and engage with your audience.

3. **Attend Speaking Engagements**: Public speaking is an effective way to showcase your expertise and build your personal brand. Wealthy individuals often engage in speaking opportunities to establish themselves as thought leaders in their industries.

    - **Action Tip:** Look for local events, webinars, or conferences where you can share your knowledge. Consider offering to speak at workshops or seminars in your area of expertise.

4. **Collaborate with Influencers**: Partnering with influencers or established figures in your industry can enhance your visibility and credibility. Collaborations can introduce you to new audiences and create valuable networking opportunities.
    - **Action Tip:** Identify influencers in your field and explore opportunities for collaboration, such as guest blogging, co-hosting webinars, or joint projects.

Maintaining Your Personal Brand

Building a personal brand is an ongoing process. Here are some strategies for maintaining and evolving your brand over time:

1. **Regularly Assess Your Brand**: Take time to evaluate your personal brand periodically. Are you still aligned with your mission and values? Are there areas where you need to improve or evolve?
    - **Action Tip:** Schedule annual or biannual brand assessments to reflect on your progress and make necessary adjustments.
2. **Stay Authentic**: Authenticity is key to a strong personal brand. Ensure that your branding efforts reflect your true self and values. People are drawn

to authenticity and being genuine fosters deeper connections.

- **Action Tip:** Regularly reflect on your actions and messaging to ensure they align with your true self. Don't be afraid to show vulnerability and share your journey.

3. **Adapt and Evolve**: As you grow and change, so should your personal brand. Stay open to feedback and be willing to adapt your brand to reflect new skills, experiences, or interests.

    - **Action Tip:** Keep a journal of your personal and professional growth. Use these insights to inform any necessary updates to your brand.

Action Step: Craft Your Personal Brand Statement

Take time to develop your personal brand statement. Consider:

- What are your core values and passions?
- What unique skills do you possess that set you apart?
- How do you want others to perceive you in your industry?

Write a brief statement that encapsulates your personal brand and serves as a guiding principle for your branding efforts.

Chapter 10: Financial Literacy and Education for Wealth Creation

The Importance of Financial Literacy

Financial literacy is the ability to understand and effectively manage financial resources. It encompasses knowledge of financial concepts, budgeting, investing, debt management, and understanding economic principles. Wealthy individuals often attribute their success to a strong foundation in financial literacy, which enables them to make informed decisions and take calculated risks.

Why Financial Literacy Matters

- **Informed Decision-Making:** A solid understanding of financial concepts empowers you to make informed decisions about budgeting, investing, and saving, ultimately leading to better financial outcomes.

- **Debt Management:** Financial literacy equips you with the knowledge to manage and reduce debt effectively, preventing it from becoming a barrier to wealth accumulation.

- **Investment Opportunities:** Knowledge of investment options allows you to identify and pursue opportunities that can grow your wealth over time.

Key Components of Financial Literacy

To become financially literate, consider focusing on these key components:

2. **Budgeting**: Budgeting is the process of creating a plan for how to allocate your income and expenses. A well-structured budget helps you track spending, save for future goals, and avoid unnecessary debt.
   - **Action Tip:** Use budgeting tools or apps to create a monthly budget. Track your income and expenses to identify areas for improvement.

3. **Understanding Credit**: Understanding how credit works is crucial for managing personal finances. Your credit score affects your ability to obtain loans, credit cards, and even rental agreements.
   - **Action Tip:** Obtain a copy of your credit report and review it for accuracy. Learn how to improve your credit score by managing payments and reducing debt.

4. **Investing Basics**: Familiarizing yourself with different investment vehicles, such as stocks, bonds, mutual funds, and real estate, is essential for building wealth. Understanding how these

investments work, and their associated risks can lead to better investment choices.

- **Action Tip:** Take an online course or read books on investing to deepen your understanding of the stock market and other investment options.

5. **Debt Management**: Learn strategies for managing and reducing debt, including prioritizing high-interest debt and understanding the impact of minimum payments.

- **Action Tip:** Create a debt repayment plan that outlines how much you will pay each month and which debts you will focus on first.

6. **Retirement Planning**: Understanding the importance of retirement savings and various retirement accounts (such as 401(k)s and IRAs) is vital for long-term financial stability.

- **Action Tip:** Start contributing to a retirement account, even if it's a small amount. Take advantage of employer matches if available.

Continuous Education and Self-Improvement

Financial literacy is not a one-time endeavor; it requires continuous education and self-improvement. Here are some strategies to enhance your financial knowledge over time:

1. **Read Financial Books**: Reading books about personal finance, investing, and wealth-building strategies can provide valuable insights and practical advice.
    - **Action Tip:** Create a reading list of highly recommended personal finance books and commit to reading one book per month.

2. **Attend Workshops and Seminars**: Participating in financial workshops and seminars can offer practical knowledge and networking opportunities. Many organizations and community centers offer free or low-cost classes.
    - **Action Tip:** Research local financial literacy workshops or webinars and attend at least one this quarter.

3. **Online Courses and Resources**: Utilize online platforms that offer courses on personal finance, investing, and money management. Websites like Coursera, Khan Academy, and Udemy have a wealth of resources.
    - **Action Tip:** Enroll in a personal finance course that interests you and commit to completing it within a specified timeframe.

4. **Follow Financial Experts**: Engage with financial experts and influencers on social media, blogs, or podcasts. Their insights and experiences can help you stay informed about current trends and strategies.
    - **Action Tip:** Identify a few financial experts to follow and set aside time each week to consume their content.

Action Step: Create a Financial Literacy Plan

Take a moment to outline your financial literacy plan. Consider:

- What areas of financial literacy do you need to improve?
- What resources will you use to enhance your knowledge (books, courses, workshops)?
- How will you hold yourself accountable for your financial education?

Write down your plan and commit to taking specific actions to improve your financial literacy.

Chapter 11: Setting Financial Goals and Creating Action Plans

The Importance of Financial Goal Setting

Setting financial goals is crucial for directing your efforts and resources toward achieving your desired financial outcomes. Goals provide clarity and motivation, helping you stay focused on your long-term objectives. Wealthy individuals often credit their success to the practice of setting specific, measurable, achievable, relevant, and time-bound (SMART) goals.

Why Financial Goal Setting Matters

- **Clarity of Purpose:** Clearly defined goals help you understand what you want to achieve financially, guiding your decisions and actions.

- **Motivation and Accountability:** Setting goals provides motivation to stay on track and accountability for your progress. It transforms abstract desires into concrete objectives.

- **Measurement of Progress:** Goals allow you to measure your progress over time, enabling you to make necessary adjustments to your plans and strategies.

Types of Financial Goals

When setting financial goals, consider categorizing them into short-term, medium-term, and long-term goals:

1. **Short-Term Goals (1 year or less)**: Short-term goals typically focus on immediate financial needs or savings. Examples include building an emergency fund, paying off a small debt, or saving for a vacation.
    - **Action Tip:** Identify one or two short-term goals that you can achieve within the next year and outline the steps needed to reach them.
2. **Medium-Term Goals (1 to 5 years)**: Medium-term goals require more planning and resources, such as saving for a down payment on a house, funding a child's education, or starting a business.
    - **Action Tip:** Write down your medium-term goals and estimate the amount of money you need to save each month to achieve them.
3. **Long-Term Goals (5 years or more)**: Long-term goals often relate to retirement planning, investing for wealth accumulation, or achieving financial independence. These goals require a comprehensive strategy and sustained effort.
    - **Action Tip:** Reflect on your long-term financial aspirations and determine the actions you need to take to achieve them.

Creating SMART Goals

To enhance the effectiveness of your financial goals, use the SMART criteria:

1. **Specific:** Clearly define your goal. Instead of saying, "I want to save money," say, "I want to save $5,000 for an emergency fund."

2. **Measurable:** Ensure your goal has measurable criteria. You should be able to track your progress. For example, "I want to increase my savings by $500 each month."

3. **Achievable:** Set realistic goals that you can accomplish based on your current financial situation. Assess whether your goal is attainable.

4. **Relevant:** Your goal should align with your overall financial objectives and values. Ensure that it matters to you and fits into your broader life goals.

5. **Time-Bound:** Set a deadline for your goal. Having a specific timeframe creates urgency and motivates you to act.

Developing an Action Plan

Once you've established your financial goals, create an actionable plan to achieve them. Consider the following steps:

1. **Break Down Goals into Actionable Steps**: Divide your goals into smaller, manageable tasks that you can tackle one at a time. This approach makes large goals feel less overwhelming.
   - **Action Tip:** For each financial goal, write down the specific actions you need to take to achieve it. For example, if your goal is to save for a vacation, your action steps might include setting a monthly savings target and reducing discretionary spending.
2. **Establish a Timeline**: Assign deadlines to each action step, creating a timeline that outlines when you will complete each task. This structure keeps you accountable and motivated.
   - **Action Tip:** Use a calendar or project management tool to track your timeline and deadlines for each action step.
3. **Monitor Progress Regularly**: Regularly review your progress toward your goals. This practice allows you to identify any obstacles and adjust your plan as necessary.
   - **Action Tip:** Schedule monthly check-ins to assess your progress. Take note of what's working and where you need to make changes.

4. **Celebrate Milestones**: Acknowledge and celebrate your achievements along the way, no matter how small. Celebrating milestones helps maintain motivation and reinforces positive habits.

    o **Action Tip:** Set up small rewards for yourself when you achieve specific milestones. This could be treating yourself to a nice dinner or taking a day off to relax.

Action Step: Define Your Financial Goals

Take a moment to define your financial goals. Consider:

- What are your short-term, medium-term, and long-term financial aspirations?
- How will you apply the SMART criteria to each goal?
- What action steps will you take to achieve them?

Write down your goals, ensuring they are clear, measurable, and time-bound, along with your action plan to reach them.

Chapter 12: Resilience and Adaptability in Financial Success

The Role of Resilience in Wealth Building

Resilience is the ability to bounce back from setbacks and adapt to challenging situations. In the world of finance, resilience is essential for overcoming obstacles, whether they are market downturns, personal financial crises, or unexpected expenses. Wealthy individuals often demonstrate resilience by learning from their failures and adapting their strategies in response to changing circumstances.

Why Resilience Matters

- **Overcoming Setbacks:** Life is full of unexpected challenges. Resilience enables you to face setbacks without losing sight of your financial goals.

- **Learning from Failures:** Resilient individuals view failures as opportunities for growth. They analyze what went wrong, learn from their mistakes, and adjust moving forward.

- **Maintaining Focus:** Resilience helps you stay focused on your long-term financial goals, even when faced with short-term difficulties.

The Importance of Adaptability

Adaptability is the ability to adjust your strategies and approaches in response to changing circumstances. The financial landscape is constantly evolving, and being adaptable allows you to seize new opportunities and mitigate risks.

Why Adaptability Matters

- **Responding to Market Changes:** Economic conditions, market trends, and consumer behavior can change rapidly. Adaptable individuals can pivot their strategies to stay relevant and capitalize on new opportunities.

- **Navigating Life Transitions:** Life events such as job changes, family growth, or health issues can impact your financial situation. Adaptability allows you to adjust your financial plans and maintain stability.

- **Embracing Innovation:** The financial world is influenced by technological advancements and emerging trends. Being open to change and innovation can enhance your investment strategies and financial management.

Building Resilience and Adaptability

To cultivate resilience and adaptability in your financial journey, consider the following strategies:

1. **Embrace a Growth Mindset**: Adopting a growth mindset means viewing challenges as opportunities for growth rather than obstacles. This perspective fosters resilience and encourages continuous learning.
    - **Action Tip:** Challenge negative thoughts and reframe setbacks as learning experiences. Ask yourself, "What can I learn from this situation?"
2. **Develop Strong Problem-Solving Skills**: Enhancing your problem-solving skills equips you to tackle financial challenges more effectively. The ability to analyze situations, identify solutions, and implement changes is crucial for resilience.
    - **Action Tip:** Practice problem-solving by analyzing past financial challenges you've faced. Identify what worked, what didn't, and how you can apply those lessons in the future.
3. **Build a Support Network**: Surrounding yourself with supportive individuals can bolster your resilience. Sharing experiences, seeking advice, and collaborating with others can provide valuable insights and encouragement.
    - **Action Tip:** Join financial groups, attend networking events, or seek out mentors

who can offer guidance and support in your financial journey.

4. **Stay Informed and Educated**: Continuously educating yourself about financial trends, strategies, and market conditions enables you to adapt your approach as necessary. Knowledge is a powerful tool in navigating financial challenges.
   - **Action Tip:** Subscribe to financial news outlets, attend workshops, and read relevant literature to stay informed about the latest developments in finance.

5. **Practice Mindfulness and Stress Management**: Financial stress can be overwhelming, making it essential to develop coping strategies. Practicing mindfulness and stress management techniques can enhance your resilience.
   - **Action Tip:** Incorporate mindfulness practices such as meditation, deep breathing, or yoga into your routine. These techniques can help you manage stress and maintain focus during challenging times.

Learning from Setbacks

Every financial journey will encounter setbacks. How you respond to these challenges is a testament to your resilience. Here are some strategies for learning from setbacks:

1. **Reflect on the Experience**: After experiencing a setback, take time to reflect on what happened. Analyze the situation and identify the factors that contributed to the outcome.
    - **Action Tip:** Write a reflection journal detailing the setback, your emotions, and the lessons learned. This practice can help you process your experiences and prepare for future challenges.
2. **Seek Feedback**: Reach out to trusted individuals for feedback on your approach and decisions. Constructive feedback can provide new perspectives and insights.
    - **Action Tip:** Schedule a meeting with a mentor or financial advisor to discuss your setback and gather their insights on how to improve your strategies.
3. **Adjust Your Strategies**: Use the insights gained from your reflection and feedback to adjust your financial strategies. Being willing to change your approach is key to resilience and adaptability.
    - **Action Tip:** Create an action plan that outlines the changes you'll make in response to the setback. Include specific

steps to implement these changes effectively.

Action Step: Cultivate Your Resilience and Adaptability

Take a moment to assess your current level of resilience and adaptability. Consider:

- How do you typically respond to financial setbacks?
- What strategies can you implement to enhance your resilience and adaptability?
- Who can you reach out to for support and guidance during challenging times?

Write down your thoughts and create a plan to cultivate your resilience and adaptability in your financial journey.

Chapter 13: Personal Development and Lifelong Learning for Wealth Sustainability

The Link Between Personal Development and Financial Success

Personal development refers to the continuous process of improving oneself in various aspects, including skills, knowledge, mindset, and emotional well-being. Wealthy individuals often prioritize personal development as a key factor in their financial success, understanding that the growth of their capabilities directly impacts their ability to create and sustain wealth.

Why Personal Development Matters

- **Skill Enhancement:** Continuous learning enables you to acquire new skills and improve existing ones, making you more competitive in the job market and better equipped to seize opportunities.

- **Adaptability to Change:** In a rapidly changing world, personal development fosters adaptability. It allows you to stay relevant in your field and respond effectively to new challenges.

- **Confidence Building:** Investing in personal growth boosts your confidence and self-esteem, empowering you to take risks and pursue your financial goals with conviction.

The Importance of Lifelong Learning

Lifelong learning is the ongoing, voluntary, and self-motivated pursuit of knowledge for personal or professional development. It encompasses formal education, self-directed learning, and experiential learning. Embracing lifelong learning is essential for maintaining financial success over time.

Why Lifelong Learning Matters

- **Keeping Up with Industry Trends:** Industries evolve, and new technologies emerge. Lifelong learning helps you stay informed about trends and advancements in your field.

- **Enhancing Problem-Solving Skills:** Continuous learning broadens your knowledge base, allowing you to develop innovative solutions to complex challenges.

- **Expanding Opportunities:** The more you learn, the more opportunities you can access, whether in your career, investments, or entrepreneurial ventures.

Strategies for Personal Development and Lifelong Learning

To foster personal development and commit to lifelong learning, consider implementing the following strategies:

1. **Set Personal Development Goals**: Define clear personal development goals that align with your financial objectives. These goals could include acquiring new skills, improving emotional intelligence, or enhancing leadership abilities.
   - **Action Tip:** Write down your personal development goals and establish a timeline for achieving them.

2. **Create a Learning Plan**: Develop a structured plan for your learning journey. Identify the resources, courses, books, or workshops that will help you achieve your goals.
   - **Action Tip:** Research and select at least three learning resources related to your personal development goals and schedule time to engage with them regularly.

3. **Embrace Online Learning Platforms**: Utilize online platforms that offer courses on a wide range of topics, from finance to personal development. Websites like Coursera, Udemy, and Khan Academy provide opportunities for skill enhancement.
   - **Action Tip:** Enroll in an online course that aligns with your personal development goals and commit to completing it.

4. **Engage in Self-Reflection**: Regular self-reflection allows you to assess your progress and identify areas for improvement. Consider what you've learned, how you've grown, and what challenges you've faced.
   - **Action Tip:** Set aside time each month to reflect on your personal development journey. Journal your thoughts, insights, and lessons learned.
5. **Seek Feedback and Mentorship**: Actively seek feedback from peers, mentors, or supervisors. Constructive feedback provides valuable insights that can guide your personal development efforts.
   - **Action Tip:** Identify a mentor in your field and schedule regular check-ins to discuss your progress and seek advice.

Cultivating a Growth Mindset

A growth mindset is the belief that your abilities and intelligence can be developed through dedication and hard work. Cultivating a growth mindset is essential for personal development and lifelong learning.

Why a Growth Mindset Matters

- **Embracing Challenges:** Individuals with a growth mindset view challenges as opportunities for growth rather than obstacles to success.

- **Persistence in the Face of Setbacks:** A growth mindset fosters resilience, allowing you to persevere through difficulties and learn from failures.
- **Increased Motivation:** When you believe in your ability to grow, you're more likely to take initiative and seek out learning opportunities.

Action Step: Commit to Personal Development

Take a moment to assess your current personal development and lifelong learning efforts. Consider:

- What personal development goals do you want to pursue?
- How will you incorporate lifelong learning into your routine?
- What steps can you take to cultivate a growth mindset?

Write down your personal development goals, you're learning plan, and specific actions you will take to commit to lifelong learning.

Chapter 14: The Significance of Giving Back and Community Contribution

The Impact of Philanthropy on Wealth

Philanthropy is the act of donating money, resources, or time to promote the welfare of others, often through charitable organizations or community initiatives. Many wealthy individuals view philanthropy as a crucial aspect of their financial journey, understanding that giving back not only benefits society but also enriches their own lives.

Why Giving Back Matters

- **Creating Positive Change:** Philanthropy plays a vital role in addressing social issues, supporting education, healthcare, the environment, and other critical areas. Wealthy individuals have the means to effect real change in their communities and beyond.

- **Building Legacy:** Giving back allows individuals to leave a legacy, creating a positive impact that can be felt for generations. Philanthropy often becomes part of an individual's identity and values.

- **Enhancing Personal Fulfillment:** Many people find deep satisfaction and fulfillment in contributing to causes they care about. Giving back fosters a sense of purpose and connection to the community.

The Benefits of Community Involvement

Community involvement goes hand in hand with philanthropy. Engaging with your local community provides opportunities to make a difference and build meaningful relationships.

Why Community Involvement Matters

- **Fostering Connections:** Engaging with your community helps build relationships and connections with others who share your values and interests.
- **Gaining New Perspectives:** Working with diverse groups of people exposes you to new ideas, experiences, and perspectives, enriching your understanding of the world.
- **Promoting Personal Growth:** Community involvement often requires stepping out of your comfort zone, which can lead to personal development and enhanced skills.

Ways to Give Back and Get Involved

If you're looking to make a difference in your community and contribute to worthy causes, consider these strategies:

1. **Volunteer Your Time**: Volunteering allows you to contribute your skills and time to organizations that align with your interests. It's an excellent way to give back and engage with your community.
    - **Action Tip:** Identify local organizations or charities that resonate with you and commit to volunteering regularly.
2. **Donate Financially**: If you have the means, consider donating a portion of your income to charities, nonprofits, or community projects that you are passionate about.
    - **Action Tip:** Research organizations and causes that align with your values and set up a monthly donation plan.
3. **Support Local Businesses**: Contributing to your local economy by supporting small businesses fosters community growth and resilience.
    - **Action Tip:** Make a conscious effort to shop locally, dine at local restaurants, and promote local events.
4. **Mentor Others**: Sharing your knowledge and expertise can significantly impact someone's life. Mentoring individuals in your field can empower them to succeed and reach their goals.
    - **Action Tip:** Reach out to local schools, universities, or professional organizations

to offer your mentorship to students or young professionals.

5. **Participate in Community Events**: Attend and support community events, such as fundraisers, fairs, or workshops. Participating in these events fosters a sense of belonging and connection.

    o **Action Tip:** Stay informed about local events and commit to participating in at least one community event each month.

Integrating Philanthropy into Your Financial Planning

Incorporating philanthropy into your financial planning can ensure that giving back becomes a consistent part of your financial journey. Here are some strategies to consider:

1. **Create a Giving Budget**: Allocate a specific percentage of your income for charitable donations and community contributions. This budget helps ensure that giving remains a priority.

    o **Action Tip:** Review your monthly budget and identify an appropriate percentage of your income to allocate to charitable giving.

2. **Establish a Donor-Advised Fund**: A donor-advised fund (DAF) allows you to make charitable

contributions and receive immediate tax benefits while deciding how to distribute the funds over time.

- o **Action Tip:** Research donor-advised funds and consider establishing one to streamline your charitable giving.

3. **Explore Matching Gift Programs**: Many employers offer matching gift programs, where they match the donations made by their employees to eligible charities. This can double your impact.

    - o **Action Tip:** Check with your employer to see if they have a matching gift program and how you can take advantage of it.

4. **Consider Legacy Giving**: Plan by including charitable bequests in your estate plan. This ensures that your values and philanthropic goals continue after your lifetime.

    - o **Action Tip:** Consult with an estate planning attorney to explore how to incorporate legacy giving into your will or trust.

Action Step: Commit to Giving Back

Take a moment to assess how you currently give back to your community and what more you can do. Consider:

- What causes are you passionate about?
- How can you integrate philanthropy into your financial planning?
- What specific actions will you take to give back and get involved in your community?

Write down your commitment to giving back, including the causes you want to support and the steps you will take to contribute.

Chapter 15: The Significance of Maintaining a Balanced Life and Well-Being

The Connection Between Well-Being and Financial Success

Well-being encompasses physical, mental, emotional, and social health. Achieving financial success is not solely about accumulating wealth; it also involves maintaining a balanced life that fosters overall well-being. Wealthy individuals often prioritize their health and well-being, understanding that personal happiness and fulfillment are essential components of their financial journey.

Why Well-Being Matters

- **Enhanced Productivity:** Individuals who prioritize their well-being tend to be more productive and focused. Good physical and mental health enables you to perform at your best in both personal and professional endeavors.

- **Reduced Stress:** Managing stress through self-care and balance helps prevent burnout and emotional fatigue, allowing you to approach challenges with a clearer mindset.

- **Improved Decision-Making:** A balanced life supports better decision-making, as individuals who prioritize their well-being are often more level-headed and resilient when faced with financial choices.

/

The Importance of Life Balance

Achieving a balanced life means allocating time and energy to various aspects of your life, including work, relationships, health, and leisure. Striving for balance is crucial for long-term success and happiness.

Why Balance Matters

- **Holistic Success:** A balanced life ensures that you nurture all areas of your life, leading to holistic success. Financial achievement alone does not equate to a fulfilled life.

- **Healthy Relationships:** Prioritizing time for family, friends, and social connections helps maintain healthy relationships, which are essential for emotional support and personal happiness.

- **Sustainable Growth:** A balanced approach to life allows for sustainable growth in both your personal and financial endeavors, reducing the risk of burnout or overwhelm.

Strategies for Maintaining Balance and Well-Being

To achieve and sustain balance and well-being in your life, consider implementing the following strategies:

1. **Set Boundaries**: Establishing boundaries between work and personal life is crucial for maintaining balance. Clearly define when your workday begins and ends and stick to those times.
   - **Action Tip:** Communicate your availability to colleagues and family members and protect your personal time.
2. **Prioritize Self-Care**: Engage in self-care activities that promote your physical, mental, and emotional well-being. This can include exercise, mindfulness, hobbies, or relaxation techniques.
   - **Action Tip:** Schedule regular self-care activities into your week, ensuring that you allocate time for activities that rejuvenate you.
3. **Cultivate Healthy Habits**: Focus on adopting healthy habits that contribute to your overall well-being, including regular exercise, nutritious eating, adequate sleep, and hydration.
   - **Action Tip:** Create a weekly meal and exercise plan that incorporates healthy choices and promotes physical fitness.
4. **Practice Mindfulness**: Mindfulness practices, such as meditation, deep breathing, or yoga, can help reduce stress and promote mental clarity. Being present allows you to appreciate the moment and enhance your overall well-being.

- **Action Tip:** Dedicate a few minutes each day to mindfulness practices and observe how it positively impacts your mindset and focus.

5. **Foster Supportive Relationships**: Surround yourself with positive and supportive individuals who uplift you. Strong relationships contribute to emotional well-being and provide a network of support during challenging times.
    - **Action Tip:** Try to connect with friends and family regularly, nurturing those relationships and providing mutual support.

Maintaining Financial Well-Being

While personal well-being is essential, it's also important to focus on financial well-being. This involves managing your finances in a way that reduces stress and promotes a sense of security.

Strategies for Financial Well-Being

1. **Create a Budget:** Develop a realistic budget that reflects your income, expenses, and financial goals. A budget helps you gain control over your finances and reduces financial stress.

- **Action Tip:** Review your current financial situation and create a budget that allows for savings, spending, and giving.

2. **Establish an Emergency Fund:** Building an emergency fund provides a financial safety net for unexpected expenses or emergencies, reducing anxiety about financial uncertainty.
   - **Action Tip:** Aim to save three to six months' worth of living expenses in a separate account for emergencies.

3. **Invest in Financial Education:** Continuous learning about personal finance, investing, and money management can enhance your financial literacy and empower you to make informed decisions.
   - **Action Tip:** Seek out resources, books, or courses that focus on financial education and commit to learning regularly.

4. **Plan for Retirement:** Prioritize retirement planning to ensure long-term financial security. Contributing to retirement accounts and understanding your options are vital for a stable future.
   - **Action Tip:** Research retirement account options and set up automatic contributions to ensure consistent savings for retirement.

Action Step: Commit to a Balanced Life

Take a moment to assess your current balance between work, personal life, and well-being. Consider:

- What areas of your life need more attention and balance?
- How can you prioritize self-care and well-being while pursuing financial goals?
- What specific actions will you take to create a more balanced life?

Write down your commitment to achieving balance, including specific goals and actions you will take to prioritize your well-being.

www.ingramcontent.com/pod-product-compliance
Lightning Source LLC
Chambersburg PA
CBHW031440210526
45464CB00005B/2279